The Let's Talk Library™

Let's Talk About Feeling Sad

Diana Star Helmer

The Rosen Publishing Group's

PowerKids Press™

New York

For Tom Owens, Don Middleton, Penny Weatherly, Miriam Landmark, Laura Dreasler,
and Bruce and Mary Walker: Remember that somebody loves you.

Published in 1999 by The Rosen Publishing Group, Inc.
29 East 21st Street, New York, NY 10010

First Edition

Book Design: Erin McKenna

Photo Credits and Photo Illustrations: p. 4 Skjold Photographs; p. 7 by Maria Moreno; p. 8 by Sarah Friedman; pp. 11, 12, 16, 19 by Carrie Ann Grippo; p. 15 by Guillermina DeFerrari; p. 20 by Seth Dinnerman.

Helmer, Diana Star, 1962–
    Let's talk about feeling sad / by Diana Star Helmer.
        p.   cm.—(The let's talk library)
    Includes index.
    Summary: Briefly discusses what makes people feel sad or depressed and some ways to handle these feelings.
    ISBN 0-8239-5193-6
    1. Sadness in children—Juvenile literature. 2 Depression in children—Juvenile literature.
    [1. Sadness. 2. Depression, Mental.] I. Title. II. Series.
    BF723.S15H45 1998
    152.4—dc21   98-3524
                                                                                    CIP
                                                                                    AC

Manufactured in the United States of America

Table of Contents

Don

Don was sad when he had to say good-bye to his grandma at the end of their visit.

"Don't be sad," Grandma said. "We had fun!"

"That's why I'm sad," Don said. "We can't play together for a long time."

"But I'll write you letters," his grandma said. That made Don feel a little better.

Don suddenly remembered. "I miss Mom!" he said. "I'm glad I'm going home."

◀ Sometimes we might feel sad about saying good-bye to someone we love.

Something's Missing

Being sad can feel like something inside you is lost or missing. Losing a baseball game can make you sad. Or maybe you wanted to see your friend today but couldn't. That can make you feel sad too. We often feel sad when things are different than we'd like them to be.

Life is always changing around us. When it changes in a way that we don't like, it can make us sad. But remembering that life changes and knowing that sometimes we might be sad and sometimes happy will make the sad times a little bit easier.

Feeling sad can make you feel alone. But there are things you can do to get yourself through a sad time. ▶

Being Sad

Being sad can be tough. When you're sad about something, it can be all you think about. You may be sad because your grandmother is sick, and all you think about is her not feeling well. This sadness can keep you from playing your favorite game or hanging out with your friends. You may not have an **appetite** (A-puh-tyt). It might be hard to sleep at night. All you can think about is what's making you feel sad. It can be hard to think about anything else until the sadness is gone.

◄ Even your favorite games may not be interesting or fun if you're very sad.

Sadness Can Hurt

Sometimes when we're sad we say our feelings are hurt. Being sad can even make your head or stomach **ache** (AYK). You might cry because you are hurt. Crying is good for you. It can help you to stop hurting.

Knowing what's wrong can help you feel better. When you're sad, ask yourself why you might be feeling bad. Learning why you're sad can make being sad a little easier. Sometimes you can even change the things that are making you sad.

Having some quiet time by yourself may help you figure out why you're feeling sad. ▶

Bodies Can Be Sad Too

When you feel sad, your body can feel sad too. Sometimes people who are very, very sad may not be able to sleep enough or eat well. Try to take care of your body. Getting enough sleep, exercising, and eating well is always important. But it's even more important when you're sad. Crying is also important in taking care of your body. Crying can help you feel **relief** (re-LEEF) from your sadness.

◀ Exercise is important for healthy bodies. And friends can make exercise more fun.

You Can Change

Maybe you're sad because your brother doesn't want to play with you. Whether you yell or ask very nicely, you can't make him play with you. You can't change how your brother feels. But you can change what you think and do. If hearing your brother say no makes you feel sad, take a break from asking him to play. Instead, ask a friend to play with you. Or play a game on your own. You can make changes to make yourself feel better. You can think and do different things to end your sadness.

14   You don't have to feel stuck in your sadness. You can make
other choices to get yourself out of a sad situation. ▶

Thinking Out Loud

Sometimes talking helps to get rid of your sad feelings. Telling someone about why you're sad helps because it lets you say out loud what is making you sad. This can help you to learn about your feelings. Sharing your sadness with someone you trust also helps you let go of a little bit of those feelings. A good listener can be your mom or dad, a **counselor** (KOWN-suh-ler), or your minister or rabbi.

◀ You can learn some good advice from talking to someone about your sadness.

A Big Sadness

Being sad is no fun. It is especially hard when the sadness lasts for a very long time. Sometimes this sadness is an illness called **depression** (de-PREH-shun).

A person with depression is usually sad for four weeks or longer. You may feel tired a lot, even too tired to do your favorite things. You might fight or cry more than usual. But you might not know why. Not knowing why you're depressed can make you feel very confused and very sad.

Remember: There is always someone who wants to help a person who is depressed. ▶

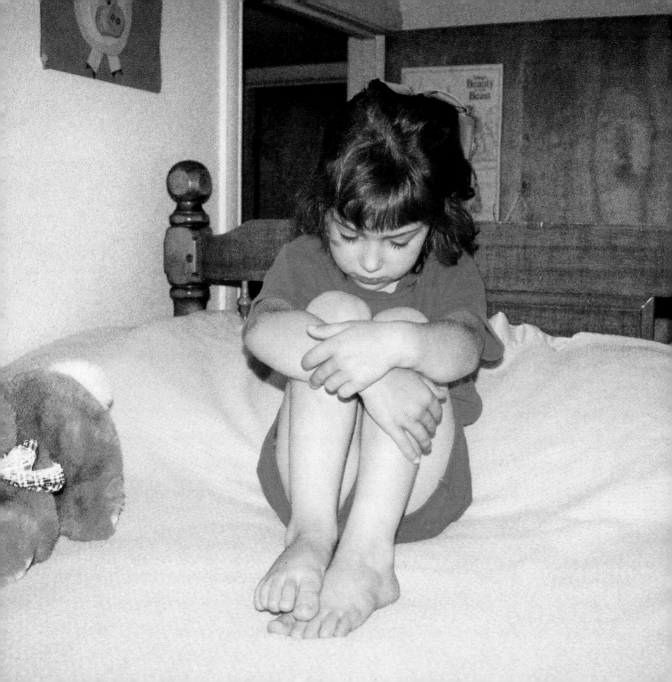

No One Has to Be Alone

A person with depression needs help, just like any person who is feeling bad. A doctor can make sure a depressed person is eating, sleeping, and exercising. Many people with depression learn to help their sad feelings by talking with **professional** (pro-FEH-shuh-nul) listeners called **therapists** (THEHR-uh-pists). Because depression is an illness, sometimes doctors give people **medicine** (MEH-dih-sin) for depression. The medicine can help people stop feeling sad.

◀ If you need to take medicine for your depression, a grown-up should always help you.

You Can Feel Happy Again

Sometimes you feel happy. Sometimes you're sad. When you are feeling sad, it can feel terrible. It may seem like you will never feel happy again. But before you can be happy, it's important to feel your sadness. You can cry if you want to. This will help you to feel your sadness and also to feel relief.

Sadness does not last forever. And even though sadness can be hard, you will feel happy again.

Glossary

ache (AYK) To be in pain.

appetite (A-puh-tyt) Feeling hungry.

counselor (KOWN-suh-ler) A person who works with others to help them with their feelings.

depression (de-PREH-shun) A sickness where a person is very sad for a long time. The sadness makes it hard for the person to work or play.

medicine (MEH-dih-sin) Something that makes a sick body feel better.

professional (pro-FEH-shuh-nul) A person who does something very well and is paid to do it.

relief (re-LEEF) To be free from pain or difficulty.

therapist (THEHR-uh-pist) A person who is trained to work with people to help them figure out their feelings.

Index